B

Provocateur of Political Satire

Clayton N. Welch

Table of Contents

Introduction

A prominent character in American media, Bill Maher is a versatile personality whose career encompasses humour, television, and political analysis. Maher, who was born on January 20, 1956, started his career as a stand-up comedian and developed his craft in bars all across the nation before moving on to television.

As the host of the late-night talk show "Politically Incorrect," which aired on Comedy Central and then ABC from 1993 to 2002, Maher became well-known. With his sharp wit and unabashed attitude to talking about touchy subjects, Maher won over many fans and became a prominent and thought-provoking figure in the field of political comedy.

Maher's current main programme, "Real Time with Bill Maher," debuted on HBO in 2003. A panel of guests from diverse backgrounds, such as politicians, journalists, and celebrities, participates in the show and has animated conversations about politics, culture, and current affairs. Under Maher's direction, "Real Time" has established a reputation for sharp criticism and a willingness to address important topics openly and humorously.

In addition to his television work, Maher has kept up his stand-up comedy career, putting out several HBO comedy specials that highlight his humorous abilities and astute observational humour. He has become a divisive character due to his propensity to push boundaries and question social conventions; he has received acclaim for his bravery as well as condemnation for his outspoken views.

Maher has never shied away from controversy in his career, frequently inviting criticism for his strong opinions on politics, religion, and social issues. Despite criticism from a variety of sources, Maher is unwavering in his dedication to intellectual integrity and free speech, using his platform to spark important conversations and inspire debate.

Beyond the entertainment industry, Maher's influence as a cultural analyst shapes public opinion and how viewers approach difficult subjects. Whether it's through his political commentary, television hosting, or stand-up comedy, Maher never fails to make people laugh, question preconceptions, and stimulate critical thought—leaving a lasting impression on American culture and the media.

Chapter 1:who is Bill Maher

Bill Maher is a multi-talented person most recognised for his roles as a political analyst, comedian, and television host. Maher, who was born on January 20, 1956, is well-known for his distinctive style of humour and sharp social criticism. As the host of the late-night discussion show "Politically Incorrect," which aired on Comedy Central and then ABC from 1993 to 2002, he became well-known.

Maher's current main programme, "Real Time with Bill Maher," debuted on HBO in 2003. In this show, Maher moderates conversations on a wide range of subjects, including politics, culture, and current affairs, with a varied group of guests. Maher, who is well-known for taking a bold stance when covering contentious issues, is regarded as a prominent and vocal voice in American media.

In addition to his work on television, Maher is a skilled stand-up comedian who has been in multiple HBO comedy specials. His comedy frequently explores political and social themes, exhibiting his astute observational abilities and cutting wit.

Maher has garnered praise and criticism for his candid views on a wide range of topics, from politics and religion to popular culture, throughout his career. Whatever one's political stance, Maher has had a major influence on public conversation because of his openness to question received wisdom and open discussions.

Apart from his work in entertainment, Maher is also a writer, having written multiple books that delve deeper into his opinions on society, politics, and religion. His work keeps people thinking and debating, solidifying his status as a well-known comic and cultural analyst.

Welcome to the World of Bill Maher

Welcome to Bill Maher's world, where insight and humour collide and wit meets wisdom. As you enter this domain, get ready to go across the social commentary landscapes, the political discourse arenas, and the comic corridors.

This is where you'll come across Bill Maher's unreserved approach to delving into the complexity of our surrounding world. With his incisive wit and unafraid criticism, Maher challenges you to confront the existing quo, refute received wisdom, and have thoughtful conversations about the matters that impact our lives.

You can see firsthand how intelligent, honest, and irreverent Maher can be when navigating the turbulent waters of modern politics and culture on his beloved late-night talk show "Politically Incorrect" and the thought-provoking conversations on "Real Time with Bill Maher."

However, Maher's universe is more than simply sarcasm and cynicism; it's also a celebration of the human condition, with humour acting as a unifying factor between divergent viewpoints and universal truths. Maher asks you to think, laugh, and accept the complexity of our world with open hearts and minds through his intelligent books and stand-up comedy specials.

Welcome to the world of Bill Maher, where finding the truth is a worthwhile adventure, politics is more than just rhetoric, and humour is more than just entertainment. Enter and get ready to be informed, amused, and maybe even challenged along the way.

Chapter 2:Early Life and Background

Born in New York City on January 20, 1956, Bill Maher grew up in River Vale, New Jersey. William Maher Sr., his father, was a radio announcer and network news editor; Julie Maher, his mother, was a nurse. Maher attended Catholic school and was raised in a Catholic home, experiences that shaped his beliefs on spirituality and religion.

Maher studied history and English at Cornell University following his high school graduation. Maher started doing stand-up comedy at neighbourhood bars while he was a Cornell student, which helped him hone his comedic abilities and find his unique voice.

After graduating from college, Maher decided to pursue a comedy career and eventually found his way into the emerging stand-up scene in New York City. His quick wit and daring take on contentious subjects won him popularity rapidly, leading to appearances on several late-night talk shows and comedy specials.

Maher's early experiences in comedy prepared him well for his later television endeavours, where he hosted his talk shows and established himself as a well-known political commentator. However, Maher's early years—growing up in suburban New Jersey and discovering his humorous voice on New York City stages—formed the basis of his profession and cleared the path for his triumph in the entertainment industry.

Childhood in New York

Bill Maher's early years were brightly coloured by his upbringing in New York City. Maher, who was born on January 20, 1956, grew up in a busy city, taking in the wide range of influences and rich cultural tapestry that surrounded him.

Maher experienced a broad range of events as a child growing up in the centre of the city, from touring famous sites like Central Park and Times Square to being fully immersed in the thriving arts and entertainment scene that dominated New York in the 1960s and 1970s.

Maher, who was raised in a Catholic home, went to Catholic school to obtain his early education and to be taught the principles and teachings of the religion. His views on spirituality and organised religion would subsequently be greatly influenced by his upbringing in a religious atmosphere.

Even though Maher grew up in a city, there were times throughout his early years when he was quiet and curious. From a young age, he developed a quick intellect and wit that would help him later in life when he became a comedian and television personality.

Maher received a multitude of experiences and influences during his early years in New York City, which helped to mould his life and profession. Maher's early years created the foundation for the fearless and outspoken voice that would eventually establish him as one of the most well-known cultural commentators in America, from the bright adrenaline of the city streets to the peaceful times of introspection.

Education and Early Influences

Bill Maher's career trajectory and outlook were significantly shaped by his early influences and schooling. Growing up in River Vale, New Jersey, Maher was exposed to the beliefs and customs of the Catholic Church while attending Catholic school. Though Maher spent a large portion of his upbringing in New York City, which has a thriving cultural scene, his education went beyond the classroom.

Maher attended Cornell University to further his studies after graduating from high school, where he studied history and English. Maher developed his love for comedy while attending Cornell, where he also practised stand-up comedy by doing stand-up routines at neighbourhood clubs. His time at Cornell gave him a strong academic foundation and acted as a springboard for his rapidly developing comedic career.

Maher was affected by a wide range of cultural and intellectual factors in addition to his official schooling. Maher took inspiration for his early career from a variety of sources, including political officials and social commentators who impacted his viewpoint and comedians who encouraged him to pursue a comedy career.

Maher's upbringing and early inspirations prepared him for his later forays into comedy and television, giving him the skills and viewpoint he needed to establish himself as one of the country's most significant cultural analysts. Maher's path to success was moulded by education, curiosity, and a tireless search for the truth and humour—from his Catholic upbringing to his time at Cornell University and beyond.

Chapter 3:Comedy Career Beginnings

Bill Maher originally dabbled in stand-up comedy while attending Cornell University, when his comedic career started to take shape. Supported by friends and the dynamic comedy culture in New York City, Maher started doing open mic nights and local clubs, where he honed his skills and honed his unique comedic style.

Maher relocated to New York City to pursue a full-time career in comedy upon his graduation from college. With his razor-sharp wit and unafraid attitude to taking on touchy subjects, he soon established himself as a rising star on the city's stand-up circuit, winning over both audiences and fellow comics.

Maher's early career in comedy was characterised by tenacity and resolve as he overcame obstacles in the entertainment sector. He performed in comedy clubs throughout the nation, honing his stuff and gaining more followers with each show.

Television producers noticed Maher's humorous abilities in the 1980s, and he went on to perform on comedy specials and late-night talk shows. He was a remarkable performer who opened doors for prospects in television and other media because of his astute observational humour and high level of intelligence.

Although Maher's comedic career would soon expand to include political commentary and television hosting, his early stand-up years were crucial to his success. Maher's career as a comedian and cultural analyst has gone a long way, starting from modest beginnings on New York City stages and culminating in national notoriety. This achievement is a tribute to his skill, tenacity, and unfailing dedication to make people laugh and think.

Stand-Up Comedy Roots

Bill Maher's background in stand-up comedy dates back to his early years spent entertaining on the lively stages of New York City. Having a natural sense of humour and wit, Maher started polishing his comic chops while attending Cornell University. He would perform his stand-up routines at open mic nights and local bars.

After graduating from college, Maher decided to pursue comedy full-time, motivated by the vibrant comedy culture in New York City. He immersed himself in the city's stand-up scene, where he made a name for himself right away with his razor-sharp observational humour and bold take on touchy subjects.

Maher's early career in stand-up consisted of numerous appearances in comedy clubs around the nation, where he polished his material and developed his sense of humour.

Both audiences and other comedians loved him for his ability to mix irreverent humour with sharp social commentary.

Maher started to appear on television, including late-night talk programmes and comic specials, as his profile in the comedy industry expanded. These changes aided in raising Maher's profile and confirming his position as a budding comic star.

Later in his career, Maher moved into political commentary and television presenting, but he never lost touch with his stand-up roots. Even now, he still does stand-up comedy, entertaining crowds with his signature humour and perceptive remarks about the world we live in.

Maher's rise from the New York City stages to widespread recognition as a comedian and cultural analyst is evidence of his skill, tenacity, and unshakable dedication to the comedy medium. Maher, who got his start in stand-up comedy, has made a lasting impression on the entertainment industry by arousing both laughter and contemplation in equal measure.

Breakthrough Moments

Over his career, Bill Maher has seen several breakthroughs that have helped him become well-known in the comedy, television, and political commentary industries.

The premiere of Maher's programme "Politically Incorrect" in 1993 marked one of his early career turning points. The programme, which debuted on Comedy Central before relocating to ABC, gave Maher a forum to have animated conversations on politics, pop culture, and current affairs. "Politically Incorrect" became a big show for Maher because of his irreverent style of addressing contentious issues and he became known as a bold pundit who wasn't hesitant to question the status quo.

"Real Time with Bill Maher": When "Real Time with Bill Maher" debuted on HBO in 2003, Maher's career took off. In his dual role as host and executive producer, Maher introduced his signature mix of intelligence and comedy to the late-night talk show format, fostering a conversation about important contemporary topics. Critically and commercially successful from the start, "Real Time" won Maher considerable praise and cemented his place as a prominent voice in American media.

Stand-Up Comedy Specials: Over his career, Maher has made several stand-up comedy specials for HBO that highlight his witty sense of observational humour and comedic abilities. These specials have been important turning points in Maher's career because they have given him the chance to interact more personally with viewers and solidify his standing as a talented comic.

Publicity and Controversial Statements: Maher's fame in the media has also been aided by his readiness to stir up controversy with his candid opinions. Maher has never shied away from speaking his views, even when it means drawing criticism from both viewers and critics. This has been demonstrated by his inflammatory remarks on his shows and his tense confrontations with guests. Even if his contentious moments have occasionally gotten him into trouble, they have also served to keep him relevant in a media landscape that is always shifting and in the public view.

Best-Selling Books: Apart from his roles in comedy and television, Maher has written several best-selling books that delve deeper into his opinions on society, politics, and religion. With the release of these books, Maher's profile as a thought-provoking and significant cultural analyst has grown beyond the entertainment sphere.

Together, these breakthrough experiences have moulded Maher's career and established him as one of the most well-known and significant personalities in American media. From his early days hosting "Politically Incorrect" to his current position as host of "Real Time," Maher has consistently pushed viewers to engage with the most important contemporary problems and think critically.

Chapter 4:Rise to Prominence

It was a combination of skill, timing, and persistence that led to Bill Maher's success in comedy, television, and political analysis.

Stand-Up Comedy: Maher first gained notoriety in New York City's stand-up comedy clubs, where he refined his humorous abilities and found his distinctive voice. His rise in the comedy industry was facilitated by his keen sense of humour and daring attitude to taking on contentious subjects, which soon attracted the attention of both audiences and other comedians.

"Politically Incorrect": In 1993, Maher's show debuted, marking a significant turning point in his career. The programme, which debuted on Comedy Central before relocating to ABC, gave Maher a forum to participate in heated discussions on politics, pop culture, and current affairs. His willingness to question received wisdom and his irreverent approach struck a chord with viewers, catapulting him to national fame as a cultural critic and political pundit.

"Real Time with Bill Maher": When "Real Time with Bill Maher" debuted on HBO in 2003, Maher achieved unprecedented success. In addition to being the presenter and executive producer, Maher also continues to push the frontiers of social commentary and political satire, addressing current events with his signature combination of intelligence and humour. With its rapid rise to popularity as a must-watch show for viewers seeking in-depth analysis and spirited debate, "Real Time" cemented Maher's place as a prominent voice in American media.

Controversial Commentary: Maher has never shied away from controversy in his career, frequently inviting criticism for his strong opinions on social issues, politics, and religion. Even if his contentious remarks have occasionally put him in hot water, they have also served to keep him relevant in a media landscape that is always shifting and in the public view.

Cultural Impact: Maher's views and observations have a significant impact on public conversation and political debate, even outside of the television medium. In addition to his stand-up comedy specials and best-selling books, he has made numerous appearances on talk shows and news programmes, solidifying his position as a thought leader and cultural icon.

Bill Maher is among the most well-known and significant personalities in American media thanks to his skill, wit, and courage to speak truth to power. From his early days performing stand-up comedy to his current position hosting "Real Time," comedian Bill Maher has always pushed listeners to think critically and participate in discussions about today's most important problems.

Television Appearances

Bill Maher has appeared on television for many years, demonstrating his flexibility as a political analyst, talk show presenter, and comedian. The following are a few of Maher's noteworthy TV appearances:

"Late Night with David Letterman": Maher frequently appeared on this venerable late-night talk programme, where he entertained audiences with his comic skills and clever repartee with host David Letterman.

"Politically Incorrect": Comedy Central and then ABC carried Maher's groundbreaking television programme from 1993 to 2002. As the host, Maher facilitated conversations on a variety of subjects with a panel of guests, winning praise from critics and a devoted fan base for his daring take on contentious subjects.

"Real Time with Bill Maher": Presented on HBO, "Real Time" has been Maher's main television show since its premiere in 2003. In this comedy-political commentary show, Maher leads conversations with people from different backgrounds, sharing his viewpoint on current affairs and social trends.

HBO has shown multiple stand-up comedy specials featuring comedian Maher, who is known for his astute observational humour and comedic skills. Through these specials, Maher has been able to deepen his connection with viewers and solidify his standing as a talented comic.

Talk Show Guest Appearances: Jimmy Fallon, "The Tonight Show Starring Jimmy Fallon," "The Late Show with Stephen Colbert," and "Jimmy Kimmel Live!" are just a few of the talk shows that Maher has frequently appeared as a guest on. He has a platform to express his opinions and joke with other hosts because he participated in these shows.

News Programmes and Documentaries: Maher has contributed his opinions on political and social topics as a guest commentator on several news programmes. Additionally, he has appeared in documentaries that cover subjects including politics, religion, and the media.

All things considered, Maher's TV appearances have been important in moulding his career and making him one of the most well-known and powerful characters in American media. From his early days on "Late Night with David Letterman" to his current position as host of "Real Time," Maher has used his perceptive commentary and irreverent humour to amuse, educate, and encourage thinking.

HBO Specials

Over the years, HBO has been treated to several funny and thought-provoking stand-up comedy specials by Bill Maher. Among his noteworthy HBO specials are the following:

"Bill Maher: But I'm Not Wrong" (2010): Maher uses his signature wit and insight to delve into a wide range of themes, including politics, religion, and pop culture.

"Bill Maher: Live from D.C." (2014): This special features Maher satirising politicians, riffing on current affairs, and analysing the absurdity of American politics. It was filmed at the Warner Theatre in Washington, D.C.

"Bill Maher: Live from Oklahoma" (2018): In this programme, Maher addresses contentious topics with his trademark combination of wit and intelligence while living in Tulsa, Oklahoma.

"Bill Maher: Live from Silicon Valley" (2021): This programme features Maher's distinct viewpoint on the nexus of politics, technology, and society, and was shot at the centre of the tech sector.Maher has established himself as one of the most important voices in comedy and political satire with these HBO specials, which all highlight his ability to handle difficult subjects with a keen sense of wit and insightful criticism.

Chapter 5:Real Time with Bill Maher

Comedian and political analyst Bill Maher hosts the weekly political chat show "Real Time with Bill Maher." When the show debuted on HBO in 2003, Maher facilitated conversations amongst a panel of guests from diverse backgrounds—politicians, journalists, activists, and celebrities—about politics, current affairs, and culture.

The structure of "Real Time" facilitates animated and frequently spirited discussions on a variety of subjects, ranging from pop culture and social issues to politics both domestically and internationally. Thanks to Maher's acute intelligence and irreverent approach, viewers can expect both entertainment and education from the show.

Maher usually opens each episode with a monologue in which he discusses the week's news and happenings in a lighthearted and frequently sarcastic manner. After the speech, Maher participates in a series of one-on-one interviews and roundtable talks with the panel of guests, questioning their viewpoints and offering his ideas.

"Real Time" includes comic sketches, pre-recorded pieces, and sporadic interviews with prominent people from the entertainment, political, and academic domains in addition to the panel discussions.

Because of its unafraid approach to taking on contentious subjects and dedication to promoting candid and open communication, "Real Time with Bill Maher" has garnered both critical praise and a devoted fan base throughout its career. The programme is still a must-watch for anybody looking for perceptive analysis and engaging discussion on today's hot-button concerns.

The Show's Genesis

Real Time with Bill Maher" has its roots in Bill Maher's former programme, "Politically Incorrect." "Politically Incorrect" began airing on Comedy Central in 1993 and then moved to ABC. Maher moderated conversations about politics, culture, and current affairs with a panel of guests.

Despite being well-liked and gaining a devoted fan base, "Politically Incorrect" was cancelled by ABC in 2002 because of contentious remarks made by host Bill Maher following the September 11 attacks. But Maher was already a powerful voice in American media because of his irreverent political commentary and willingness to take on touchy subjects.

After HBO cancelled "Politically Incorrect," Maher collaborated with the network to create a new show that would expand on the structure of his former show while providing more creative latitude and flexibility. "Real Time with Bill Maher," the outcome, made its HBO debut in 2003.

"Real Time" kept the main components of "Politically Incorrect," such as host Maher and the panel debate style of current affairs. But, without the limitations of network television, Maher was able to explore political satire and social criticism even further after moving to HBO.

"Real Time with Bill Maher" has always been distinguished by its irreverent humour, razor-sharp wit, and daring take on contentious subjects. The programme attracted viewers right away and won praise from critics for its incisive commentary and stimulating discussions.

A mainstay of political and cultural criticism even in modern times, "Real Time with Bill Maher" provides viewers with a special mix of education and amusement as he and his panel of guests analyse the week's news with wit, irreverence, and intellect.

Concept and Format

The idea behind "Real Time with Bill Maher" is to provide thoughtful and animated conversations on politics, society, and current affairs in a forum. Below is a summary of the main components of the show:

Host and Guests Panel: Bill Maher is the show's host and moderator. Maher participates in conversations with a group of guests from diverse backgrounds, such as politicians, journalists, activists, and celebrities, in each episode. The panellists' varied points of view add to the depth and scope of the conversation.

Maher usually opens the show with a monologue in which he provides his witty and frequently incisive analysis of the previous week's news and happenings. The tone for the remainder of the programme is established by Maher's irreverent humour and sharp satire in his monologues.

Panel conversations: After the monologue, Maher has a series of one-on-one interviews and roundtable conversations with the panel of guests. Social issues, pop culture, politics both domestically and internationally, and other subjects are covered. Maher's job is to lead these conversations by challenging his guests' viewpoints and offering his own observations.

Audience Involvement: "Real Time" frequently hosts audience participation, with Maher taking questions and comments from viewers during specific show segments. This exchange gives the proceedings a further degree of spontaneity and engagement.

Comedy Segments and Interviews: "Real Time" includes pre-recorded comedy segments, comedy sketches, and sporadic interviews with prominent personalities from the entertainment, political, and academic domains in addition to the panel discussions. These parts offer lighthearted relaxation while enabling a more thorough examination of particular subjects or problems.

In general, the idea and structure of "Real Time with Bill Maher" are intended to promote thoughtful analysis, impassioned discussion, and amusing commentary on today's most important topics. For anyone looking for intelligent and provocative conversations on politics and culture, the show is still a must-watch because of its unique blend of irreverence, humour, and intelligence.

Notable Segments and Guests

Over the years, "Real Time with Bill Maher" has included several noteworthy segments and has welcomed a diverse array of prominent guests. The following are some of the noteworthy guests and segments:

New Rules: One of the show's most recognisable parts, "New Rules" includes Maher making several amusing and frequently biting observations on various facets of politics and society. Each episode's high point is these monologues, which present Maher's distinct perspective on contemporary affairs and cultural fads.

Overtime: "Real Time" frequently carries on online with an "Overtime" part that comes after the main panel talks. In this segment of the show, Maher and his guests delve deeper into the subjects covered in the main broadcast by holding additional conversations and answering questions from the audience.

"Real Time" Interviews: Maher interviews prominent figures from politics, entertainment, and academics one-on-one in addition to the panel discussions. These interviews enable in-depth examination of particular subjects and provide viewers with a glimpse into the viewpoints of prominent personalities.

Guest Panels: Maher regularly organises groups of people to discuss various points of view on a given topic or subject. These panels provide viewers with a variety of viewpoints on difficult subjects and can spark lively discussions.

Sketches and Comedies: "Real Time" offers pre-recorded sketches and comedies that offer lighthearted reprieve and humorous comments on current affairs. These parts inject humour into the show's discussions and frequently feature Maher or special guest comedians.

Notable Visitors: Politicians, journalists, activists, and celebrities are just a few of the notable people that "Real Time" has had the pleasure of hosting over the years. Salman Rushdie, Elizabeth Warren, Neil deGrasse Tyson, Barack Obama, and Bernie Sanders are just a few of the notable guests who have been on the show.

In general, viewers looking for perceptive analysis and lively conversation on today's most important problems should not miss "Real Time with Bill Maher" due to its blend of funny commentary, thought-provoking debates, and a variety of viewpoints.

Chapter 6:Controversies and Criticisms

Throughout his career, Bill Maher has faced several problems and complaints due to his outspoken and frequently provocative opinions. Here are a few noteworthy examples:

Remarks on September 11: Following the terrorist attacks on September 11, 2001, Maher made a contentious statement on his programme "Politically Incorrect," asserting that the perpetrators were not cowards who had carried out the atrocities. ABC cancelled the show as a result of the controversy caused by the remarks.

Remarks against Islam: Maher has come under fire for his direct and frequently severe criticism of Islam, especially concerning how it treats women and what is seen as its intolerance. His remarks have drawn criticism from civil rights groups and Muslim communities who claim that they are encouraging Islamophobia.

Racial Insensitivity: Maher has come under fire on multiple occasions for saying racially offensive things. Using a racial term in an interview with Senator Ben Sasse in 2017 caused a stir. Though Maher later expressed regret for the comment, it sparked new conversations about racism in America and Maher's part in maintaining negative perceptions.

Immunisation Scepticism: On his show, Maher has voiced his scepticism regarding vaccines and provided guests with a forum to spread conspiracy theories against them. Maher's platform is criticised for facilitating the dissemination of false information and undermining public health initiatives to avoid diseases that can be prevented by vaccination.

Treatment of Guests: Maher has come under fire for talking over and interrupting his guests a lot, as well as for his aggressive interviewing approach. There have been awkward and heated discussions on broadcast as a result of guests accusing Maher of being contemptuous or condescending.

Political Bias: Maher has come under fire for allegedly having a liberal bias in his analysis and for picking and choosing which political leaders and ideologies to criticise. Critics contend that Maher's politicised style erodes his authority as a dispassionate analyst and exacerbates the division in political discourse.

Although Maher has received praise from some areas for his willingness to speak his mind and challenge conventional thought, it has also made him a target for controversy and criticism. Maher continues to be a well-known and significant personality in American media despite these scandals, provoking discussion and debate on a variety of topics.

Political Outspokenness

Bill Maher is well-known for being vocal about political matters and for frequently using his platform to provide insightful analysis and scathing criticism of the status of American politics. Here are a few salient features of Maher's political activism:

Partisan Criticism: When he feels that a party is not acting in the best interests of the nation or upholding principles, Maher is not hesitant to criticise both Democrats and Republicans. Regardless of party, he routinely criticises politicians for their ineptitude, duplicity, and caving into special interests.

Progressive Views: Although Maher considers himself to be a liberal, he is well-known for his propensity to oppose liberal dogma and retaliate against what he perceives to be overly politically correct behaviour in progressive communities. Maher's progressive stances frequently coincide with concerns about LGBTQ rights, healthcare reform, environmental preservation, and civil liberties.

Religious Criticism: Maher views organised religion—especially Islam and Christianity—as the root of intolerance, irrationality, and injustice. He has been vocal in his criticism of these faiths. He has been outspoken in his defence of secularism and free speech, frequently at odds with conservatives and religious authorities on matters like the right to an abortion, the rights of the LGBTQ community, and religious fundamentalism.

Support for Free Speech: Maher is a fervent supporter of free speech and has spoken up for people's rights to voice divisive or unpopular viewpoints without worrying about retaliation or censorship. He has argued that free speech and debate are necessary for a robust democracy and has spoken out against political correctness and cancel culture.

Opposition to War and Interventionism: Maher has made a strong case against American military operations conducted overseas, especially in the Middle East. He has advocated for a more cautious foreign policy that emphasises diplomacy and humanitarian aid over military action and opposed the Iraq War.

Advocacy for Climate Change: Maher is a fervent supporter of taking action against climate change. He frequently emphasises the pressing need to solve environmental issues and chastises corporations and governments for not placing a higher priority on sustainability and renewable energy efforts.

All things considered, Maher's political candour is a reflection of his dedication to opposing established hierarchies, upholding progressive principles, and encouraging candid discussion of matters that have a bearing on society's future. Even while Maher's opinions might be divisive at times, his courage to speak truth to power has won him a devoted fan base and solidified his position as one of the country's most important political pundits.

High-Profile Disputes

Throughout his career, Bill Maher has been embroiled in several high-profile confrontations, many of which have been sparked by his provocative remarks and outspoken opinion. Here are a few noteworthy examples:

"Politically Incorrect" Was Cancelled: In 2002, ABC cancelled Bill Maher's show "Politically Incorrect" due to remarks he made on the September 11 terrorist attacks. When Maher said that the terrorists weren't cowards, there was a lot of negative reaction, and the show was eventually cancelled.

Disputation over Racial Slur: In 2017, Maher caused a stir by using a racist slur in an interview with Senator Ben Sasse on "Real Time with Bill Maher." After commenting, Maher quickly came under fire, with many criticising him for being insensitive and racist. Although Maher expressed regret for the remark, it sparked new conversations about racism and race in America.

Conflicts with Politicians: Over the years, Maher has publicly clashed with several politicians, most notably former President

Donald Trump. Maher has been a strong opponent of Trump's actions and ideas, frequently mocking and denouncing the previous president with his platform.

Conflicts with Religious Leaders: Maher's vocal critique of organised religion has brought him into conflict with communities and religious leaders. Maher's comments about Islam and Christianity in particular have drawn accusations that he is encouraging Islamophobia and anti-religious hostility.

Statements about Islam that Aroused Controversy: Muslim groups and human rights organisations have denounced Maher's remarks regarding Islam. Maher has come under fire for allegedly inciting anti-Muslim sentiment and disinformation, which has sparked contentious discussions and demonstrations.

Conflicts with Hollywood Icons: Over the years, Maher has also engaged in public conflicts with several Hollywood icons, primarily centred around topics about free speech and political correctness. Maher disagrees with individuals in the entertainment business who support more sensitive and inclusive rhetoric because of his critique of identity politics and cancel culture.

Although Maher's propensity to stir up controversy has made him a target for criticism, it has also solidified his standing as a fearless pundit who won't back down when speaking his opinion. Despite the disagreements and conflicts, Maher is still a well-known and significant personality in American media.

Chapter 7:Political and Social Commentary

Bill Maher is known for his political and social commentary, which is distinguished by his keen humour, unwavering honesty, and readiness to question accepted wisdom. The following are some major ideas and ideas in Maher's commentary:

Political Satire: Maher is well-known for his scathing use of humour in his political satire, which targets politicians, commentators, and political organisations. His irreverent style of politics frequently highlights the absurdity and hypocrisy in the political system, which makes him popular with viewers looking for lighthearted commentary on current affairs.

Cultural Criticism: Maher's analysis touches on a wider range of cultural topics, such as popular culture, media, and religion than just politics. He doesn't hesitate to take on contentious subjects and question accepted social mores; his thought-provoking observations frequently ignite a conversation.

Civil Liberties and Free Speech: Maher is an outspoken supporter of both civil liberties and free speech, arguing that the First Amendment should be upheld as well as the value of free discussion and debate. He has been an outspoken opponent of attempts to muzzle dissident voices, political correctness, and censorship.

Religious Criticism: Maher views organised religion—especially Islam and Christianity—as the root of intolerance, irrationality, and injustice. He has been vocal in his criticism of these faiths. He has been a strong supporter of the separation of church and state and has urged for further secularism.

Environmental Advocacy: Maher regularly emphasises the necessity of tackling climate change and supporting renewable energy programmes. He is a fervent supporter of environmental sustainability and protection. He has demanded more funding for green technology and chastised businesses and politicians for doing too little to address environmental problems.

Maher is an advocate for women's rights, racial equality, and LGBTQ rights. She is a supporter of social justice and equality. He has utilised his platform to spread awareness of structural injustices and inequality and has been outspoken in his support of progressive causes.

All things considered, Maher's political and social commentary is distinguished by its brilliance, humour, and unflinching candour. Whether he's criticising religious doctrine, mocking politicians, or pushing for social justice, Maher's commentary always makes people stop and think, makes them debate and challenge the status quo.

Key Issues Addressed

In his political and social commentary, Bill Maher covers a wide range of important topics, reflecting his diverse interests and worries about the status of the world. The following are some of the main topics Maher regularly discusses:

Politics and Government: Maher focuses on issues including electoral politics, government corruption, and the impact of money in politics. He provides sharp analysis and critique of political figures, parties, and policies.

Civil Rights and Free Speech: Maher is an outspoken supporter of civil rights, such as the right to privacy, freedom of the press, and freedom of speech. He regularly criticises attempts to silence alternative views, political correctness, and censorship.

Religion and Secularism: Maher challenges religious dogma, superstition, and intolerance as an outspoken opponent of organised religion. He frequently draws attention to the perils of religious fanaticism and extremism while arguing in favour of secularism and the separation of church and state.

Climate Change and Environmentalism: Maher emphasises the critical need for environmental sustainability and protection and is a strong supporter of action on climate change. He demands more funding for conservation and renewable energy initiatives and attacks corporations and politicians for their inaction on environmental issues.

Maher is an advocate for women's rights, racial equality, and LGBTQ rights. She is a supporter of social justice and equality. In addition to calling for changes to address systemic racism, sexism, and discrimination, he denounces systemic injustices and inequities.

Foreign Policy and War: Maher provides an analysis of U.S. foreign policy, covering arms sales, military operations overseas, and diplomatic ties with other nations. He favours a more measured approach to international relations, placing more emphasis on diplomacy and humanitarian assistance than on military action.

Healthcare and Public Health: Maher talks about public health and healthcare policy, including topics such as prescription drug pricing, access to care, and the value of preventative care. He backs initiatives to strengthen public health infrastructure and is an advocate for universal healthcare coverage.

These important topics are some of the most important problems that society is currently experiencing, and Maher's analysis serves to highlight them, get people thinking, and inspire action. When it comes to social conventions, religious views, or political leaders, Maher's criticism always acts as a call to action for his audience to become involved with the topics that matter.

Impact on Public Discourse

Bill Maher's outspoken comments and daring approach to taking on contentious subjects have had a tremendous influence on public discourse, influencing discussions on politics, culture, and society. Here are a few ways that Maher has impacted popular opinion:

Provocative Commentary: Maher has gained notoriety in American media due to his openness to express his opinions and question received knowledge. His astute analysis, irreverent humour, and cutting wit have managed to break through the political propaganda and provide viewers with a different take on the day's news.

Energetic Debate: On his programme "Real Time with Bill Maher," Maher hosts spirited discussions on a variety of subjects. Maher promotes conversation and interaction on important topics by bringing together speakers with a range of experiences and perspectives. This helps viewers have a deeper comprehension of difficult subjects.

Power Critique: Maher is well-known for his criticism of political figures, establishments, and hierarchies of power. His opinion exposes injustice, corruption, and hypocrisy in the political system by holding people in positions of power accountable. Maher inspires viewers to question authority and demand transparency from their elected authorities by being prepared to confront the status quo.

Support of Free Speech: Maher is a strong supporter of open discourse and free speech, frequently opposing attempts to stifle dissident voices and repression. His support of First Amendment rights and dedication to encouraging free discussion have contributed to the advancement of an intellectually diverse and free-expression culture in public discourse.

Emphasising Social Concerns: Maher frequently discusses social concerns in his comments, including injustice, prejudice, and inequality. Maher promotes action to address systemic problems in society by drawing attention to these issues and elevating the voices of marginalised communities.

Maher's effect is not limited to politics; it also encompasses a wider range of cultural trends and events. His analysis of entertainment, social media, and popular culture shapes public opinion and attitudes, which in turn affects the larger cultural zeitgeist.

Ultimately, Maher's influence on public conversation may be attributed to his fearless dedication to confronting the current quo, telling the truth to power, and promoting viewer involvement and critical thought. Maher's observations, whether they are mocking politicians, challenging religious doctrine, or promoting social justice, act as a spur for change and an inspiration to those who want to change the world.

Chapter 8:Personal Life

In addition to being well-known for his sardonic humour and insightful analysis, Bill Maher has a fascinating private life off-screen. A peek into his private life is provided here:

Early Years: Maher was raised in River Vale, New Jersey, after being born in New York City on January 20, 1956. He majored in history and English at Cornell University.

Relationships: Maher has never been married, although, over the years, he has been romantically associated with several well-known women. In interviews, he frequently avoided answering questions about his relationships because he was known to keep his personal life private.

Interests & Hobbies: Maher enjoys a wide range of interests and pastimes outside of his work in media and entertainment. He has written multiple books on politics, religion, and culture and is an enthusiastic reader. Maher also likes to travel, see live shows, and hang out with friends.

Philanthropy: Maher is well-known for his charitable endeavours, which include backing initiatives that protect animal rights, the environment, and civil liberties. Throughout the years, he has made donations to numerous organisations and charities, utilising his position to spread awareness of significant social concerns.

Health & Well-Being: Maher has been transparent about his dedication to maintaining good health and well-being, promoting a balanced diet and frequent exercise. He has advocated plant-based nutrition for its advantages in terms of both health and the environment, and he eats a vegetarian diet.

Criticism & Controversies: Maher has occasionally faced criticism from both audiences and commentators due to his outspokenness and controversial remarks. Maher is unwavering in his resolve to speak his opinion and question the current quo despite the backlash.

All things considered, Maher's personal life is a reflection of his complex personality and interests, ranging from his academic interests to his charitable work. Although Maher's scathing commentary on television may be his most well-known contribution, his private life provides a glimpse into the man behind the headlines.

Relationships and Family

Although Bill Maher has maintained a relatively low profile, the following information about his relationships and family is known:

Maher does not currently have children and has never been married.

Romantic Relationships: Throughout his career, Maher has maintained romantic ties with several well-known women, including the actresses Ann Coulter and Coco Johnsen.

Maher does, however, want to keep information on his private relationships private and avoid answering queries about his love life in interviews.

Family History: William Maher Sr., a radio announcer and network news editor, and Julie Maher, a nurse, were the couple who gave birth to Maher. Kathy Maher is the name of his sister. Maher was raised mostly by his mother after his parents separated when he was a small child.

tight ties: Despite not having a conventional family of his own, Maher keeps tight ties with acquaintances and colleagues in the entertainment sector. He works closely on projects and socialises outside of work with his close-knit group of friends and acquaintances.

Because Maher likes to keep the specifics of his relationships and family life hidden, his personal life is still mostly mysterious. Maher's attention to his activism and career, despite this privacy, is well-documented, demonstrating his commitment to his work and his love of social and political criticism.

Hobbies and Interests

Outside of his work life, Bill Maher, who is well-known for his insightful analysis and cutting wit, enjoys a variety of pastimes and interests. Maher has the following interests and pastimes:

Reading: Maher enjoys reading a lot and has a strong interest in politics, history, and literature. He is recognised for reading to stay up to date on current affairs and concerns, and he has frequently referenced books as inspiration for his comedies and commentaries.

Stand-Up Comedy: Outside of his television profession, Maher has a deep love for comedy. He is a skilled stand-up comedian who has appeared in theatres and comedy clubs all over the nation. Maher is still on the road frequently, entertaining crowds with his sharp observations and lighthearted insights.

Travel: Maher likes to go on trips and discover new places. Maher has a history of travelling extensively for business or pleasure, taking in the sights, sounds, and viewpoints of different civilizations.

Sports: Maher enjoys playing a lot of sports, especially baseball. He has been seen supporting his favourite team, the New York Mets, by going to games.

Political action: Maher is quite active in political action and advocacy outside of his entertainment business. His passions include social justice, environmental preservation, and civil rights. He utilises his position to advocate for topics he believes in and to increase awareness of them.

Healthy Living: Maher eats vegetarianism and is dedicated to his health and well-being. He stresses the value of looking after one's physical and emotional well-being and promotes healthy living and frequent exercise.

In general, Maher's interests and pastimes show his wide range of inclinations and his insatiable curiosity. Maher has a voracious appetite for knowledge and embraces life with excitement, whether he's reading a book, acting on stage, or fighting for social change.

Chapter 9:Legacy and Influence

In the fields of humour, television, and political commentary, Bill Maher has left a lasting and profound legacy. Here are some salient features of Maher's impact and legacy:

Political comedy forerunner: Maher is recognised as a trailblazer in the field, having opened the door for a new wave of comedians who utilise comedy to address important social and political concerns. Numerous comedians have been inspired by his caustic style and daring treatment of contentious subjects to use their platforms for activism and social criticism.

Provocateur and Thought Leader: Maher has gained recognition as a thought leader who is both provocative and influential thanks to his remarks on "Politically Incorrect" and "Real Time with Bill Maher". His keen sense of humour, perceptive analysis, and willingness to question the current quo have established him as a reliable source in American media, impacting political discourse and influencing public opinion.

Supporter of Free Speech: Maher is a fervent supporter of free speech and candid discussion. He frequently rebels against attempts to stifle opposing viewpoints, political correctness, and censorship. His support of First Amendment rights and dedication to encouraging free discussion have contributed to the advancement of an intellectually diverse and free-expression culture in public discourse.

Cultural Icon: Maher's influence goes beyond politics to include more general cultural phenomena and trends. His analysis of popular culture, religion, and social issues has shaped public opinion and attitudes, impacting the larger cultural zeitgeist.

Activism and Philanthropy: Maher is a political activist and philanthropist in addition to being a vocal figure in the entertainment industry. His passions include social justice, environmental preservation, and civil rights. He utilises his position to advocate for topics he believes in and to increase awareness of them.

Inspiration for Upcoming Generations: Maher's contributions to comedy, television hosting, and politics will serve as a source of inspiration for upcoming actors and activists. For those who want to change the world, his bravery, brilliance, and dedication to speaking truth to power serve as an inspiration.

All things considered, Maher's impact and legacy are defined by his unwavering integrity, astute humour, and commitment to furthering significant social and political objectives. Maher's influence on American media and public debate is evident, regardless of whether he is criticising religious ideas, taking aim at political leaders, or calling for social justice.

Contributions to Comedy

In the comedy world, Bill Maher has made a great impact, especially in the areas of social commentary and political satire. Bill Maher made the following significant contributions to comedy:

Political Satire: Maher is well known for his incisive use of humour to parody political figures, commentators, and establishments. He is regarded as one of the best political comedians of his generation because of his skill in cleverly and wryly ridiculing the absurdity of American politics.

Fearless Commentary: Maher has distinguished himself in the comedy industry by his willingness to take on contentious subjects and voice his opinions without concern for retaliation. He is an unashamed and daring pundit who is not hesitant to question authority, challenge political correctness, or tackle taboo themes.

Blending Humour and Journalism: Maher's distinctive approach to combining humour and journalism has made it more difficult to distinguish between news and entertainment media. His programmes, "Politically Incorrect" and "Real Time with Bill Maher," give viewers a forum for thoughtful conversations on politics, culture, and current affairs while also making them laugh.

Cultural Commentary: Maher provides insightful analysis on a broad range of cultural topics, including as popular culture, media, and religion, in addition to politics. He has gained repute as a cultural critic for his ability to wryly and intelligently analyse and critique societal conventions and tendencies.

Stand-Up Comedy: Maher's ability to provide funny and thought-provoking comedy on stage is demonstrated in his stand-up comedy specials. His talks frequently touch on social criticism, political views, and personal tales, providing audiences with a special fusion of humour and wisdom.

Inspiration for Upcoming Generations: Maher's contributions to humour have served as an inspiration for satirists and comedians in subsequent generations. Those who want to utilise humour as a vehicle for social and political commentary might take inspiration from his bold approach to comedy and his dedication to speaking truth to power.

All things considered, Bill Maher's contributions to humour have had a profound impact on the genre and have shaped our perceptions of society, politics, and culture. Maher continues to push the limits of humour and satire while challenging and entertaining audiences with his daring criticism and razor-sharp wit.

Influence on Media and Politics

Because he holds a special place at the nexus of humour, journalism, and political analysis, Bill Maher has a huge impact on the media and politics. Here are some salient features of Maher's impact:

Creating a Public Dialogue: Bill Maher's television programmes, "Politically Incorrect" and "Real Time with Bill Maher," have developed into significant forums for forming public dialogue about societal issues, politics, and culture. Maher helps to define and contextualise important problems through his sharp comments and insightful interviews, which affect how people understand and discuss them.

Encouraging Civic Involvement: Maher's analysis of current affairs and political topics stimulates viewers' political consciousness and civic involvement. Maher gives viewers the tools they need to participate in the political process more actively and intelligently by offering a platform for thoughtful debate and discussion.

Holding Power Accountable: Maher promotes openness in government through his bold approach to confronting political figures and establishments. He contributes to the public's perception of politicians as being truthful and accountable by being willing to confront spin and disinformation with pointed questions.

Exposing injustice and Hypocrisy: Maher frequently calls out corruption, injustice, and hypocrisy in society and politics in his comments. Maher advocates for social and political change by bringing attention to topics like corporate influence, wealth inequality, and civil rights violations. This helps to mobilise the public and promote consciousness of these concerns.

Swaying Public Opinion: Maher has a significant impact on public opinion on social media and other digital channels in addition to his television broadcasts. His opinions and observations are frequently shared and discussed online, affecting political discourse and influencing public opinion in real-time.

Establishing the Agenda: With his monologues and panel discussions guiding the news cycle and impacting coverage in other channels, Maher's shows frequently set the agenda for political conversation in the media. Maher contributes to the narrative shaping around significant political subjects by drawing attention to them and presenting them in an entertaining and captivating manner.

All things considered, Bill Maher's impact on the media and politics may be attributed to his capacity for thought-provoking, education, and entertainment. Maher is a vital force in influencing public opinion, holding authority figures responsible, and encouraging civic involvement both within and outside of the US through his activism and analysis.

Conclusion

Due to his distinctive fusion of intelligence, humour, and social commentary, Bill Maher has had a profound and wide-ranging influence on comedy, the media, and politics. Throughout his professional life, Maher has distinguished himself as a daring provocateur who pushes the limits of public debate and challenges received wisdom.

From his early days as a stand-up comedian to his ground-breaking work on television, Maher has constantly used his position irreverently, witty, and with insight take on the most important topics of the day. His adeptness at fusing humour with biting political commentary has won him a strong fan base and established him as a reliable voice in American media.

Maher's contribution to comedy in popularising political satire as a kind of entertainment is among his greatest achievements. With programmes like "Politically Incorrect" and "Real Time with Bill Maher," he has shown how comedy can educate and enlighten viewers about difficult political subjects. Maher's courage to tackle taboo topics and undermine established power structures has encouraged a new wave of comedians to utilise comedy to remark on social and political issues.

In addition to his impact on the comedy industry, Maher has shaped the media environment and how we absorb news and information. His shows have given viewers a much-needed respite from the soundbite-driven coverage of mainstream media by acting as a venue for thoughtful discussion and debate. Because of Maher's dedication to free speech and honest discussion, his audience has developed a culture of critical thinking and intellectual curiosity.

Maher has had an equally significant impact on politics. His unrelenting criticism of public officials and political organisations has contributed to the accountability of those in positions of authority and brought attention to topics that may have gone unnoticed. Millions of people have been motivated to become more involved and active citizens by Maher's support of social justice, environmental preservation, and civil freedoms.

Maher's reputation as a trailblazer in comedy, media, and politics is certain as his career develops further. Maher continues to be an essential and crucial voice in American public life, whether he is criticising politicians, questioning religious doctrine, or pushing for social change. Maher has earned his standing as one of the most significant personalities of his generation with his unwavering commitment to speaking truth to power, his razor-sharp wit, and his fearless honesty.

54721028R00044